HORSEFIELD TORTOISES AS PET

Complete owners guide to horsefield tortoise training, care, reproduction, management and many more included

ALBERT A. NELSON

Table of Contents

Introduction

Horsfield tortoises, also known as Russian tortoises, are native to the desert regions of Central Asia and have unique characteristics that make them unique and beloved companions. Welcome to the wonderful world of Horsefield Tortoises, where these reptiles have won the hearts of reptile enthusiasts and pet owners alike.

This comprehensive guide explains in depth what it takes to care for a Horsfield tortoise and provides vital advice to ensure your pet's health and happiness. From creating a suitable environment and understanding behavior to dealing with common health issues, we plan to reveal the secrets of responsible Horsfield tortoise ownership.

Learn about a comprehensive nutritional guide to caring for these amazing animals and the different stages of their life cycle, from cute hatchlings to robust adults, and environmental enrichment techniques to keep your Horsfield Tortoise happy and healthy.

You'll gain a better understanding of these gentle creatures as we discuss bonding, socialization, and substrate selection. Whether you're a seasoned reptile enthusiast or a beginner, this guide should give you the knowledge and skills you need to provide the best care for your Horsfield's Tortoise.

Join us on this educational adventure to learn how to build a strong and lasting relationship with your Horsfield Tortoise.

Chapter 1

Horsfield Tortoise Care: Essential Tips for a Happy Pet

Horsfield tortoises, scientifically known as Agrionemys horsfieldii or Testudo horsfieldii, have become popular as pets due to their small size, popularity and hardy nature. These reptiles are native to the arid regions of Central Asia and require special care to ensure their happiness and safety in captivity.

1. Understanding the natural environment:
Horsfield tortoises are not adapted to arid and semi-arid environments such as the steppes of Central Asia, so it is important that you recreate this natural habitat for them, which you can do using a terrarium or an outdoor enclosure on sandy soil. The soil they find in their birthplace.

2. Heat and light;

Horsfield tortoises require proper temperature and lighting maintenance, with a hatch kept between 90 and 95°F (32 and 35°C) and a cooler kept between 75 and 85°F (24 and 29°C). Full-spectrum UVB lighting is required for the turtles' calcium metabolism and overall well-being.

3. Correct enclosure setting:-

Create a safe and comfortable environment for your turtle, a large house with hiding places and a shallow bowl of water for bathing. You can also add natural materials to their habitat, such as logs and pebbles, to help engage their imagination.

4. Proper diet:

Your Horsfield Tortoise needs a balanced diet that includes foods like kale, collard greens, and dandelion greens, as well as calcium and vitamin D3 supplements.

5. Keeping hydrated;

Always make sure fresh, clean water is accessible, as well as shallow water for diving, which is beneficial for shell health and hydration.

6. Frequent veterinary visits:

To monitor your turtle's health, schedule regular exams with a veterinarian who specializes in pets. Early detection of any abnormalities allows for prompt intervention and treatment.

7. Management and Socialization:

Horsefield tortoises are not as social as other pets, but they still need gentle socialization; Handle them gently so they get used to your presence, but encourage them often because they need time alone.

8. Substrate Selection:-

A mixture of topsoil, coconut coir and cypress mulch can be used to create a surface that closely replicates the burrowing and burrowing characteristics of their natural habitat.

9. Environmental improvement;
Providing your turtle with new experiences and different environments will help keep him or her happy and healthy. Enriching the environment includes exploring hiding places, climbing buildings, and toys.

10. Estimate Lemerat
Investigate and appreciate the breeding responsibilities of Horsefield tortoises; Breeding should be done with great care for the safety of adults and any young.

11. Recognizing and Addressing Health Issues:
Carefully observe the appearance and behavior of your turtle; Abnormalities in the shell, changes in appetite or

apathy are all symptoms; If you notice any symptoms, contact your veterinarian immediately.

Vacation and seasonal changes;
Because hibernation mimics their natural behavior and can be beneficial if done correctly, it's a behavior that occurs in the wild, so it's important to do your research and follow the right steps if you want to let your field tortoise hibernate.

13. Ownership of Liability;
The Horsefield tortoise requires a long-term commitment; Understand their unique needs and be prepared for a lifespan that can span decades, good ownership habits can help these fascinating reptiles live long and healthy lives.

14. Important Legal Notices:-

Before purchasing a Horsfield tortoise, be aware of any legal requirements or restrictions that may apply in your area. Certain states may have laws that restrict the ownership of certain reptiles.

15. KEEPING OF RECORDS;

Keep a journal of your turtle's health, diet, and behavior for future reference and to notify your veterinarian properly if your turtle becomes ill.

In conclusion, providing the necessary care for your Horsfield's Tortoise requires special knowledge, dedication and a true love for these amazing reptiles. By understanding and implementing these tips, you are not only ensuring your pet's physical health, but also contributing to their overall satisfaction and well-being. Remember that each turtle is an individual and you can tailor their care to meet their individual needs by looking at their b.

Chapter 2

Exploring the world of Horsefield turtles involves more than just providing a suitable habitat. It also includes understanding their complex behavior. As individual reptiles, Horsfield's tortoises exhibit behaviors that convey important messages about their overall health, well-being, and general condition.

1. Search and Forage:
Horsfield turtles are naturally curious about their environment, and use their powerful legs to move around their habitats in search of food and good places to dive. This activity allows them to connect with their surroundings and stimulate their minds.

2. Temperature controls and sun exposure

Horsfield tortoises die because they regulate their temperature by exposing themselves to sunlight, and their basking behavior provides insight into their overall well-being.

3. Tunneling and Excavation:-

Digging and burrowing are common activities for Horsfield's tortoises, especially when burrowing or hiding. By providing enough surfaces in their cages, you can encourage this habit and help them satisfy their instincts and improve their overall health.

4. Social behavior:

Horsefield tortoises are not social animals by nature, but they can exhibit certain territorial tendencies if kept in groups, so monitoring is important to reduce hostility and maintain a stable environment.

5. Communicating through body language:

Being aware of these non-verbal cues can help create a setting that reduces stress and creates a sense of security for the turtle.

6. Retreat and hide;

Horsfield's tortoises retreat into their shells when they feel scared or threatened as a natural defense mechanism to help them avoid potential attacks and creating hiding places in their cages is crucial to making them feel safe.

7. Interaction with objects;

Adding pebbles, logs or toys to their environment will stimulate the turtle's curiosity. You can push objects around, engage with them, or use them as climbing frames. The presence of different materials will improve their environment and develop their mind.

response to environmental changes;

Horsfield tortoises are creatures of habit, and are uncomfortable with unexpected changes in their environment. Whether it's a new living space configuration or a change in temperature, simply watch their reactions to make sure they're adapting.

9. Behavior of marriage and courtship:-
Male Horsfield Tortoises may exhibit head-tossing or turning during mating, which sheds light on the breeding cycle and is useful for anyone considering breeding these tortoises.

10. Seasonal and Activity Level Differences:
Horsfield tortoises, like other reptiles, exhibit seasonal behavioral changes, such as being more active in the colder months, and understanding these fluctuations can help adjust care routines such as feeding and lighting.

11. Problem Solving and Cognitive Skills:

Horsfield tortoises are not considered particularly intelligent, but they can solve problems, walk, hide, and identify their owners. They can also be trained to demonstrate their cognitive abilities by presenting puzzles or challenges.

12. Health Indexes:-

Sudden changes in a turtle's activity level, feeding habits, or general behavior should be watched closely. Frequent observations allow early detection of potential health problems, facilitating appropriate veterinary care.

13. Sleep and Sleep Patterns:

Horsefield tortoises have unusual sleeping habits; They are usually busy all day and have less rest at night. If your turtle is thinking about hibernating, it's important to understand natural cues and create a suitable environment to help him mimic his natural behaviors.

14. Interpersonal Relationship:-

While Horsfield tortoises are not known for being highly social, they can get used to human presence and handling through frequent interactions and positive experiences with your tortoise.

15. Increase in life expectancy and behavioral changes:

Given the longevity of Horsefield tortoises, their behavior may change with age; It is important to recognize these behavioral changes and adjust treatment so that your turtle can live a happy and healthy life.

In conclusion, learning about the behavior of Horsefield Tortoises is an exciting adventure that requires persistence, keen observation, and respect for the peculiarities of their movements. By exploring their world and learning the meaning behind each behavior, you will improve their quality of life and form a close bond with these amazing reptiles.

Chapter 3

Equine enclosures: designing the perfect environment

Starting the process of building a Horsfield Turtle dream home is a much more rewarding endeavor than providing a place to live. It involves learning about their inner needs, instincts, and the fine balance needed to maintain their physical and mental health.

1. Size of enclosure:-

If the weather permits, consider outdoor enclosures that allow more space and exposure to natural sunlight.

2. Substrate Selection:

A substrate made of topsoil, coconut husks and cypress mulch encourages burrowing and burrowing behaviors while maintaining good moisture levels and providing a comfortable environment for the turtle.

3. Increase in temperature;

Enclosures should have a temperature gradient to allow the turtle to regulate its body temperature: the warm part should be between 75 and 85 degrees Fahrenheit (24 and 29 degrees Celsius) and the basking area should be between 90 and 95 degrees. Fahrenheit (32 and 35 degrees Celsius). Frequent temperature monitoring ensures a comfortable and healthy environment.

4. UVB light;

Full-spectrum UVB lighting is essential for Horsefield Tortoises to promote calcium metabolism and prevent metabolic bone disease. Place UVB lamps in the hatch so that the turtle has access to this light source most of the day. Replace UVB bulbs regularly to maintain their functionality.

5. Concealers and Covers:

It is important for Horsfield tortoises to have enough hiding places to relieve stress and stimulate natural behaviors. These can be constructed from natural materials such as logs, stones, or professionally prepared hides.

6. Water Bodies:-

Because Horsfield turtles cannot swim, they use a shallow bowl of water for drinking and diving. Make sure the bowl is easily accessible and cleaned regularly to keep it clean. Keeping an eye on their hydration levels is very important, and having a separate place to soak can help prevent dehydration.

7. Exit elements

Adding climbing structures to the enclosure will add variety and encourage natural behavior in the turtles. Placing flat rocks, logs, or specially designed climbing structures encourages exploration and exercise, improves the environment, and provides opportunities for natural exercise.

8. Grassland and edible plants;

Tortoise-safe plants such as hibiscus, dandelions, and other grasses can be included in the yard to allow Horsfield tortoises to participate in their natural foraging habits.

9. Dining Stations:-

Set up special feeding stations in the compound to help maintain hygiene and provide a balanced and varied diet, as well as a more integrated approach to reducing food contamination and simplifying nutritional monitoring.

10. Environmental improvement;

To keep Horsfield tortoises cognitively engaged, add different elements to the enclosure, such as rotating and introducing new objects, changing the arrangement regularly, or building a burrow with loose mats.

11. Reliable Enclosure Design:

As Horsfield Tortoises are adept diggers, it is important to ensure that the enclosure is secure and escape-proof, and you should regularly inspect the enclosure for defects or wear on the enclosure material.

12. Plant turtle-friendly plants;

Choose and research turtle-safe and non-toxic plants before planting immediately in the yard; This improves the appearance of the fence by providing more hiding places and natural foraging opportunities.

13. Keeping the order:

Regular cleaning and grooming are essential to the health of the Horsfield Tortoise. Clean the area, clean the water bowl regularly and remove uneaten food as soon as possible. Do a more thorough cleaning once a month to remove bacteria and dirt deposits.

14. Paying attention to behavioral signs:
Understanding the needs of the turtle should pay close attention to how it behaves in the enclosure. If you hide or run away from a certain place frequently, changes in the environment may be necessary. By designing the enclosure based on the turtle's behavioral cues, you can create a stress-free living environment.

15. Seasonal Differences:-
If your Horsfield Tortoise's temperature and daylight hours vary naturally, you may want to consider making seasonal changes to their environment by adding more

heat or adjusting lighting hours during the winter months. .

In conclusion, creating a suitable home for Horsfield's Tortoises requires a comprehensive strategy that takes into account their temperaments, physical needs and psychological health. As responsible caregivers, it is our responsibility to create an environment that not only satisfies children's basic needs, but also allows them to express their natural tendencies, so that children can live happy and meaningful lives.

Chapter 4

Horsfield tortoises are herbivores with unique nutritional needs and require a broad and balanced diet to thrive. In this comprehensive feeding guide, we'll examine the nutritional requirements of Horsefield Tortoises, including appropriate foods, feeding schedules, and necessary supplements to ensure a healthy and happy life for your beloved companion.

1. Natural Wild Diet:
Understanding the nutritional needs of Horsfield tortoises in captivity requires an understanding of their natural diet in the wild. Their energy and health are built on this plant-based diet.

2. Leafy greens;

Leafy greens are an important part of the Horsefield Tortoise's diet as they are rich in fibre, vitamins and minerals. Include a variety of greens in their diet: Turn around He turned around and turned around. Most of their daily meals .

3. Grass and hay;

Horsfield tortoises need high-fiber hay and grass to keep their digestive systems healthy, and Bermuda grass hay and timothy hay are excellent choices. These fibrous substances help the bowels to move and prevent diseases such as constipation.

4. Edible Plants and Flowers:

Edible weeds and flowers such as dandelions, clover, hibiscus flowers, and nasturtiums are safe choices for Horsfield tortoises. These supplements encourage natural foraging tendencies by providing a variety of nutrients.

5. Create:

Include a small amount of vegetables in the diet to increase the variety of vitamins. Cucumbers, zucchini, bell peppers and carrots are good options. But avoid vegetables rich in oxalates, such as kale and spinach, because too much of them can cause calcium binding.

6. Fruit:

Fruits like strawberries, watermelon and papaya are high in sugar and should only be served as a treat. Fruit should be used as a supplement rather than a main food source because too much sugar can lead to obesity and other health problems.

7. Calcium supplement;

Calcium is important for the growth and maintenance of the Horsfield tortoise's shell, as well as for the overall health of its bones. Sprinkle vitamin D3-rich calcium supplements on leafy greens and vegetables, or give turtles bones to chew on to avoid metabolic problems.

8. Phosphorus management;

Maintain a healthy ratio of phosphorus to calcium in your diet, as too much phosphorus can interfere with calcium absorption. Limit your child's phosphorus-rich foods, such as nuts and seeds, and focus on providing calcium and a variety of rich foods.

9. Avoid high protein foods:

High protein diets are not necessary for Horsfield tortoises, and too much protein can cause kidney problems. Cut down on high protein foods like meat and vegetables and instead focus on getting the right amount of fiber, vitamins and minerals.

10. Dining Schedule:-

Prepare a regular meal plan to limit the amount of nutrients taken. While young tortoises may need to eat more often, adult Horsfield tortoises normally benefit from daily feedings. Keep track of their weight and adjust the portion size accordingly.

11. Get plenty of water

Horsefield tortoises need to drink enough water to stay healthy, so provide them with a small bowl of water to drink from as they get moisture from their food. Additionally, watering your turtle with lukewarm water a few times a week will promote hydration and prevent dehydration.

12. Seasonal Differences:-

Be aware that your turtle's diet varies with the seasons. They are more active in the summer months, so you may notice an increase in hunger. Adjust feeding schedules and amounts accordingly. Metabolism can slow down in winter, so you need to feed them less.

13. Avoid using poisonous plants.

Learn about plants that are poisonous to turtles and make sure you don't eat them. Common garden plants that can be dangerous include ivy, rhubarb and many flowers. Do your research before adding more plants to the nest.

14. Track your weight and fitness:

Horsfield Turtle Keep a close eye on your weight and physical condition; A healthy turtle should look like a small rubbery object with a nicely rounded shell. If you notice weight loss or changes in the appearance of your shell, consult a veterinarian immediately.

15. Food Cycle Schedule:-

Implement a rotating meal plan to increase variety and prevent nutritional deficiencies. Alternate between different herbs, vegetables, and edible weeds to ensure a variety of nutrients, similar to how you would eat in the wild.

16. Breeding factors:

When breeding Horsfield tortoises, it is especially important to examine the nutritional needs of gravid (or pregnant) females. Supplement with calcium and make dietary modifications to improve egg production and effective reproduction.

17. Veterinary tests:-

Regular veterinary check-ups are required to ensure your turtle's overall health and that their nutritional needs are met. A veterinarian specializing in reptiles can advise on dietary changes based on the age, health and special needs of the tortoise.

18. Updates and Educational Materials:

Keep up with advances in reptile nutrition and care. A better understanding of the health of Horsefield tortoises and new research findings may lead to improved feeding recommendations. Find information by participating in reptile forums, literature and veterinary resources.

In conclusion, feeding your Horsfield tortoise is a complex part of ownership that requires knowledge, commitment and attention to detail. By eating a varied and balanced diet that matches their natural foraging habits, they improve their longevity, energy and overall well-being. Adjust their diet to suit their needs, pay attention to their needs and enjoy knowing you are giving your Horsfield Tortoise the best possible diet.

Chapter 5

This comprehensive guide examines common health problems encountered by Horsfield tortoises and provides information on their causes, symptoms, and practical methods of prevention and treatment.

1. Respiratory infections;

- Causes: Inadequate temperature and high humidity are two prominent environmental conditions associated with respiratory problems in the Horsefield tortoise, although respiratory problems can also be caused by bacterial or viral infections.

- Symptoms of respiratory infection include shortness of breath, runny nose, open mouth breathing and fatigue.

- Prevention and Treatment: Keep your turtle at an appropriate temperature, provide adequate ventilation, and keep it away from drafts. If you have trouble breathing, contact your veterinarian immediately. Both supportive care and antibiotics can be used in treatment.

2. Decay Shells:

- Causes: When a turtle's shell is constantly exposed to a moist environment, it can become infected with bacteria or fungi, causing the shell to rot. Injuries, inadequate hygiene and lack of hygiene can all cause shell decay.

- Signs of shell decay are discoloration, fluid spots on the shell, and an unpleasant odor; In severe cases, the bone may become infected.

- Prevention and Treatment: Make sure your turtle has access to a dry, clean, dry enclosure and clean the enclosure regularly to maintain good hygiene. See a veterinarian for proper diagnosis and appropriate treatment, which may include antibiotics or antifungals.

3. Metabolic bone disease (MDD)

- Metabolic bone disease is caused by calcium and vitamin D3 deficiency. It can also be caused by insufficient UVB exposure, an unbalanced diet, or improper supplementation.

- Symptoms of MBD include tremors in the limbs, difficulty moving, and abnormalities or irregularities in the shell.

- In severe cases, veterinary intervention such as supportive care and calcium injections may be required. Prevention and treatment methods include appropriate UVB exposure, calcium supplements, and a balanced, high-calcium diet.

4. Parasitic infections;

- Internal parasites such as worms and protozoa can affect horseshoe crabs, and parasitic infections can occur through contaminated food, water, or contact with sick animals.

- Symptoms of parasite infection include changes in stool appearance, weight loss, diarrhea and fatigue.

- Prevention and Treatment: Provide clean food and water, maintain a clean environment, and practice good hygiene. Frequent animal examination of feces can help detect and treat parasitic infections.

5. Problems with the eyes;

- Injuries, illnesses or underlying medical conditions can all cause eye problems in Horsfield Tortoises. A stressful environment or lack of moisture can be a problem.

- Symptoms of eye problems include discharge, excessive tearing and swelling, red or cloudy eyes.

- Maintain adequate hydration, keep the area clean, and watch for signs of eye disease. Consult a veterinarian for proper diagnosis and appropriate treatment, which may include antibiotic eye drops.

6. Egg binding;

- Female Horsfield tortoises can struggle to lay eggs for a variety of reasons, such as low calcium levels, dehydration, or improper bathing conditions.

- Symptoms of ovulation include insomnia, stress, anxiety, or digging without ovulation.

- Prevention and Treatment: Provide a dignified surface as well as a suitable nesting area. Make sure you eat calcium-rich foods and stay hydrated. Egg binding is a potentially dangerous condition, so if in doubt, seek veterinary care immediately.

7. Dehydration;

- Dehydration in turtles can be caused by water shortages, drought conditions, or diseases.
- Symptoms of dehydration include dry eyes, fatigue, dry skin, and unusual urine patterns.
- Treatment and Prevention: Provide a drinking bowl with shallow water and continuous flooding. Make sure the humidity level in the garden is appropriate. In cases of severe dehydration, veterinarians may be asked to administer fluid therapy.

8. Influence:

- When a turtle ingests substrate or other indigestible material, the digestive tract becomes blocked, resulting in no effect. This may be due to improper food consumption or not having a healthy diet.

- Symptoms of exposure include bloating or flatulence, loss of appetite and fatigue.

- Provide a decent amount of nutrients to promote digestion, and be careful not to include anything that won't spoil the turtle's food. Consult a veterinarian for diagnosis and treatment plan; In severe cases, surgery and/or hydration may be required.

9. Overgrown claws and beak:

- Causes: A turtle may have an enlarged beak and claws if it does not have food scraping or is unable to find surfaces that naturally degrade these structures.

- Symptoms include difficulty feeding, excessive beak growth, and untrimmed, curled nails.

- Prevention and Treatment: Provide clean surfaces with natural materials such as rocks. Watch for ingrown beaks and claws and trim them regularly or seek professional help from a veterinarian.

10. Stomatitis (spot rot).

- Stomatitis, or inflammation of the oral tissues, can be caused by injury, malnutrition, or bacterial or fungal infections.

- Symptoms of stomatitis include swelling, discharge and chewing.

- Prevention and Treatment: Keep your tongue clean, maintain a balanced diet, and watch for any abnormalities. Consult a veterinarian for proper diagnosis and treatment, which includes the use of antibiotics or antifungal drugs.

11. Sleep problems:-

- Causes: Sleep-related health problems can occur if the turtle is not adequately prepared for sleep or the environment is not maintained.

- Symptoms of insomnia include difficulty falling asleep, difficulty moving, and inability to wake up.

- Prevention and Treatment: Make sure you are properly prepared for any scheduled naps, including cooling off and water from time to time. Monitor hibernating turtles and seek immediate medical attention if problems occur.

12. Feature enhancements:

- Causes: Changes in behavior, such as frequent hiding, lack of activity, or changes in eating habits, can indicate health problems.

- Symptoms: Although they can vary widely, behavioral changes are often related to stress, pain, or problems.

- Prevention and Treatment: Monitor your turtle's behavior closely and intervene quickly if it changes. Consult a veterinarian for a comprehensive health evaluation and place your pet in a consistent and suitable environment.

13. Damages and Incidents;

- Accidents, breakdowns, and interactions with other animals are all potential causes of trauma and injury. Consideration should also be given to environmental hazards or incorrect treatment.

- Symptoms of trauma include obvious sores, itching, and behavioral changes after an accident.

- Prevention and Treatment: Maintain a safe environment, avoid handling that may injure or distress people, and monitor potential hazards. Consult a veterinarian for a thorough examination and treatment.

14. Dystocia, or difficulty producing eggs:

- Dystocia is a condition in which a female turtle has trouble laying eggs. This is typically caused by egg size concerns, handicaps or a lack of acceptable nesting sites.

- Dystocia is characterized by stress, sleepiness and frequent urination without ovulation.

- Prevention and Treatment: Provide a suitable nesting site, ensure adequate calcium intake, and monitor nesting activity. If dystocia is suspected, seek immediate veterinary assistance for evaluation and intervention.

15. Increased stress levels

- Stress can be caused by various reasons, bad management, insufficient environmental conditions or environmental changes.

- Symptoms of stress include changes in activity level, decreased appetite, and behavioral changes.

- Keep the environment consistent, try not to create too much disturbance, and handle the turtle carefully and gently. To avoid prolonged stress, recognize and resolve stressful situations as soon as possible.

Finally, proper husbandry, careful attention, and early detection and resolution of potential problems are all critical to the health of the horseshoe crab. A healthy diet, regular veterinary care and a comfortable environment all contribute to longevity and overall health. Being aware of the common health issues mentioned above and taking preventative measures can help ensure that your Horsfield's Tortoise lives in captivity and provides you with years of enjoyment and companionship. Always seek the advice of an experienced reptile veterinarian for professional guidance tailored to your turtle's unique needs.

Chapter 6

Horseshoe Tortoises: From Hatching to Adulthood

Agrionemys horsfieldii, commonly known as Testudo horsfieldii, is a fascinating animal whose life goes through many stages of growth and development. As they grow from hatchlings to adults, these reptiles change in size, behavior and preferred habitats. It is very important to understand each step in order to provide the best possible care and ensure the safety of these strong and beloved animals. In this comprehensive guide, we'll explore the several stages of the Horsfield tortoise's life cycle, emphasizing the unique characteristics, requirements, and critical components of each stage.

1. Egg incubator:

The egg-laying process begins the life cycle of the Horsefield Tortoise. Female turtles usually choose a separate nest to lay their eggs. The eggs are buried in the ground to protect them from predators and the environment. The eggs are round and leathery in shape. Although it varies, the incubation period is usually 60 to 90 days.

2. Incubation:

When the incubation period is over, the young turtles hatch from the eggs. The thin, pliable shell that chicks hatch from eventually hardens. Hatching is a critical stage in the life cycle, and hatchlings have an innate ability to bury their hatchlings.

3. Dimensions and Appearance:

Hatchling Horsefield turtles are very rare, averaging 1.5 to 2 inches in length. Their shells pale in comparison to the dynamic and distinct patterns that emerge as they age. These juvenile turtles have endearing characteristics such as large eyes and an exposed face.

4. Investigation and Action:-

Hatchlings are inquisitive by nature and are curious about their surroundings. They tend to alternate between rest and exploration time. Providing a safe and enjoyable environment is essential to nurture their natural tendencies and encourage healthy development at this stage.

5. Diet and nutrition;

Horsfield Hatchling turtles have specific nutritional requirements. Their growth and shell production depend on a diet rich in leafy greens, finely chopped vegetables and calcium supplements. Ensuring proper nutrition during this developmental stage is the first step to a healthy and happy turtle.

6. Residential configuration:-

Hatchery enclosures should be properly proportioned to the size of the animals in them. A small, safe area with a shallow bowl of water, hiding places and a temperature for baking is required. The soft ground and the general environment should imitate the comfort and safety experienced in the cottage.

7. UV-B Exposure:

Providing adequate UVB lighting is essential for hatching Horsfield tortoises. Exposure to UVB rays is required for proper calcium metabolism and strong and healthy shell development. It is very important to place UVB lamps so that the chicks receive the UVB rays they need.

8. Annual Growth Rate:

During its early life, the Horsfield tortoise grows at a relatively rapid rate. A good environment, access to UVB light, and proper nutrition all contribute to healthy growth. Looking at the turtle's weight and size can provide valuable information about their overall health.

9. Converting to a larger enclosure:
As it grows, the Horsefield Tortoise will grow its first container. Moving to a larger area allows for more stimulating features, increased movement, and continued exploration. This update takes into account their number and level of activity.

10. Adolescence;
Adolescence is characterized by continuous growth and development. Horsfield tortoises are more docile and may exhibit mature habits at this time. Adolescents, who are not adults, have increased independence and may begin to be careful about what they eat.

11. Dietary changes:

Adolescent Horsefield tortoises may need to change their diet to satisfy their appetite. A varied and balanced diet consisting mainly of leafy greens and vegetables is important for their overall health. Calcium supplementation is still important for shell growth.

12. Shell design;

During puberty, the Horsefield tortoise's shell hardens and develops characteristic markings. The overall appearance of the shell is improved, and the bone plates are more visible. Nutrition and UVB sun exposure are critical components of this ongoing process.

13. Social organization;

As they grow, horseshoe crabs may exhibit distinct social behaviors. Although people are not naturally sociable, interactions can occur, especially if they live together. Keeping track of these variables is critical to maintaining a suitable home and preventing adversities.

14. Mature fertility;

Horsfield tortoises reach sexual maturity between 5 and 8 years of age, although this can vary depending on genetics, habitat and diet. Males display certain behaviors during courtship, such as head butting, circling, or trying to mount females. Females may participate in nesting behavior.

15. Nest building and rearing:-

Female Horsfield tortoises may engage in nest-related activities such as digging and searching for suitable sites while sexually mature. A separate area should be provided with adequate space for females to lay eggs. Understanding the reproductive cycle is critical for individuals considering starting a family to make the best reproductive decisions.

16. Hatchery and Egg Planting;

Females bury their eggs in their beautifully designed nests. These eggs last 60 to 90 days, which is comparable to the time it takes for the first chicks to form. To ensure the effectiveness of this reproductive phase, a suitable environment for nesting and egg laying must be created.

17. Parental care is limited:

Compared to other species, tortoises do not show a high level of parental care. After the eggs are laid, the females may not be directly involved in caring for the young. The survival and development of the hatchlings is largely determined by the surrounding environment and the proper care provided by the turtle keeper.

18. Long-term expansion and sustainability;

Horsfield tortoises can live for decades and grow to adulthood if properly cared for. An adult turtle's shell is stronger, more fully developed, and has a different color and pattern. Due to their long lifespan, these reptiles require long-term care from their caretakers.

19. Home care in later life:

Adult Horsfield tortoises require constant and stimulating environments to be cared for. Providing a balanced diet, ensuring proper UVB exposure, and monitoring for any signs of health problems are part of this. Regular vet check-ups are becoming increasingly important to ensure their long-term health.

20. Environmental improvements;

Adult Horsfield tortoises may exhibit some environmental adaptations. They will learn to navigate their dens, use crevices, and seek cover when necessary. By learning about their preferences and behaviors, caregivers can build a space that honors their inner needs.

21. Old Age and Life Span:

As they age, horseshoe crabs may lose energy. Understanding aging is critical to changing their care system. These turtles have an amazing and extended lifespan, allowing them to live well into their 50s or even longer with proper care.

In summary, the Horsefield Tortoise's life cycle is a fascinating journey that includes stages of growth, maturation, and adaptation. From the small and delicate hatchlings that emerge from their eggs, these reptiles fascinate fans with their diverse behaviors and activities. The overall well-being of these strong and charming animals depends on listening attentively at all levels, understanding their needs, and adapting the environment appropriately. Appreciating each step of their life cycle ensures a positive and lasting bond with these beautiful reptilian companions for those who care for them.

Chapter 7

Horsfield tortoises (Agrionemys horsfieldii or Testudo horsfieldii) need a stimulating environment to thrive. These hardy reptiles are native to the deserts of Central Asia, and the right habitat design helps them mimic their natural behavior in captivity. This comprehensive guide covers a wide variety of techniques and components to improve Horsfield's Tortoise habitat enrichment, stimulating activity, mental stimulation, and overall well-being.

1. Enclosure layout and dimensions:-

Appropriately sized enclosures are the basis of environmental enrichment. Horsfield tortoises are small in size but require a large habitat. An enclosure size of at least 4 feet by 8 feet is recommended for an adult turtle, allowing enough space for the turtle to move around, explore, and exhibit its natural tendencies.

2. Different elements:

A heterogeneous substrate improves sensory performance in Horsfield's tortoises. A suitable base for digging and drilling is composed of earth, coconut husk and cypress mulch. These different surfaces encourage natural movement and contribute to the overall prosperity of their surroundings.

3. Climbing Structures:

A common misconception is that tortoises only live on land, but Horsfield's tortoises enjoy climbing and exploring high places. Add logs, flat rocks, or specially constructed ramps to encourage vertical movement. These structures not only improve their environment, but also provide opportunities for physical activity.

4. Hide areas and covers;

Hides and shelters should be constructed to reduce stress and allow turtles to exit when necessary. Natural materials adorning the enclosure include wood, stone and commercial leather. These hiding places provide shelter and mimic the natural behavior of turtles in the wild.

5. Excavation Site:-

Because Horsfield Tortoises enjoy digging, providing them with some space to do so will greatly enhance their habitat. If their natural digging behavior takes them, they can dig in a sand hole or any other loose area. This energizing activity promotes both mental and physical activity.

6. Land for grazing and edible plants;

Including edible plants in the yard encourages natural grazing and adds beauty. Turtle-friendly plants include grasses, hibiscus, and dandelions. Create a grazing area to encourage foraging, which supports a variety of foods and mental stimulation.

7. Temperature areas with temperature differences;
Baking areas with heat exchangers should be provided so that Horsefield tortoises can maintain temperature control. A temperature between 90 and 95 degrees Fahrenheit (32 and 35 degrees Celsius) is ideal for baking because it promotes healthy metabolism and digestive function. Make sure the cool side temperature is 75-85°F (24-29°C) so the turtle can comfortably regulate its body temperature.

8. Features related to water include:
Although Horsfield turtles cannot swim, they use shallow water to bathe and drink. A water feature such as a shallow dish or low-sided container adds movement

to the enclosure. The water is safe for turtles to drink and swim in, which is good for their overall health.

9. Placement of driving object:-

Add new items to the enclosure by rotating it regularly to improve the environment. This may include adding new objects, changing stones, or adjusting hiding places. The arrangement of spinning objects keeps things interesting and stimulates the turtle's interest.

10. Natural hides and caves;

Imitating the natural burrowing movements of Horsefield tortoises makes them feel safer and enriches their experience. Incorporate natural hides and burrows by systematically planting rocks, logs or soil mounds to encourage digging and exploration.

11. UVB radiation from natural sunlight:

Horsfield tortoises need direct sunlight or UVB lamps. Exposure to UVB rays is important for calcium metabolism and overall health. Place UVB lamps above hatches so that turtles can access this important light source. If they are placed outdoors, make sure they get access to both sunny and shady areas.

12. Interactive Kitchen Sinks:
Create interactive eating stations to turn mealtimes into learning opportunities. Spread food around the enclosure to encourage the turtle to explore and search on its own. This will satisfy their natural appetite and keep them from getting bored with regular diet.

13. Signs of Perception:-
To appeal to different senses, use sensory stimulation. Because turtles are visual and tactile learners, it's fun to experiment with different textures, colors, and shapes in their environment. Examples include different types of

pebbles, rough surfaces and even safe objects with different textures.

14. Introducing Turtle Friendly Toys:-

Although not as playful as other pets, tortoises can be curious about certain things. Tortoise-safe toys such as textured objects or hard rubber balls should be introduced. These artifacts invite investigation and engagement.

15. Eating Obstacles and Puzzle Games:

Games and puzzles are included to enhance the eating experience. To encourage the turtle to solve problems and conduct more active foraging, food can be buried in the hide or placed in a puzzle feeder.

16. Seasonal Differences:-

Consider changing the enclosure to meet the turtle's current needs. Because turtles are more active in the warmer months, providing extra reinforcement, such as new items or rearranged ingredients, will keep them interested. Adjustments include lighting and temperature changes.

17. Mirrored or mirrored surfaces:

Give the enclosure a mirror or other reflective surface to give it visual appeal. Turtles may be curious about adding something new to their environment or interested in their own reflection. Monitor their responses to ensure they are not stressed.

18. Interacting properties of water:

Create an interactive water feature for the turtle using a shallow tub or tray. Adding floating objects or edible plants can increase the beauty of this area. Turtles have a different sensory experience when splashing around or exploring water features.

19. Response and Observation:

See how the turtle behaves and how it responds to enrichment. If certain items or items seem to capture their interest, consider introducing more of the same items or items in the future. Responding to personal preferences enables custom enrichment of environments.

20. Environmental changes due to aging:

Understand that Horsfield tortoises' needs and preferences may change as they age relative to their environment. As they grow, it becomes increasingly important to provide opportunities for greater movement, exploration, and environmental complexity. Changes should be made to reflect their changing needs and habits.

21. Participating and Viewing:

While Horsfield Tortoises are not as smart as other pets, spending time watching and interacting with each other can help strengthen their bond. Respect each individual's personality and preferences and enjoy seeing them in their improved environment.

22. Enrichment audit normally:
Conduct periodic optimization audits to evaluate the effectiveness of features and positioning. Decide how the turtle interacts with different things and make the necessary changes to make the habitat interesting. Enrichment should be a dynamic and ever-changing aspect of prison.

23. General Health Examination:-
The overall health and well-being of Horsefield Tortoises is linked to environmental enrichment. Creating a dynamic environment promotes behavioral satisfaction,

mental and physical activity, and a more holistic approach to their care.

In summary, creating better habitat for Horsfield's tortoises requires purposeful habitat planning, behavioral analysis, and ongoing monitoring. Caregivers can ensure these hardy reptiles have a happy and enjoyable life in captivity by providing them with a variety of components that support their basic tendencies and habits. It is critical to create a dynamic, diverse and ever-changing environment that supports their physical and mental well-being and allows them to express their individuality and character.

Chapter 8

Choosing the best Substratum for your equal companion

Choosing the right replacement for your Horsefield Tortoise (Agrionemys horsfieldii or Testudo horsfieldii) is an important part of providing a safe and enjoyable home. It performs a variety of functions, including activating natural behaviors, aiding in temperature regulation, and maintaining your turtle's overall well-being. In this detailed guide, we'll look at the features to consider when choosing a replacement for your Horsfield Tortoise, as well as the different options available, so you can make an informed decision that best suits your reptile's needs.

1. Consideration for natural habitat:

Understanding the natural environment of Horsfield's tortoises is essential to choosing the appropriate substrate. These turtles live in desert areas with sandy or sandy soil. In captivity, simulating similar settings can help establish a familiar and comfortable environment for your turtle.

2. Adequate drainage:

One of the most important purposes of the elements is to provide proper drainage. If kept in extremely humid conditions, Horsfield tortoises are prone to respiratory problems. Choose a surface that allows water to flow well, preventing moisture from accumulating in the fence.

3. Softness and porosity;

Horsfield tortoises love to burrow and burrow. Choose a smooth and soft surface that allows them to have a natural character. Coconut husks, cypress mulch, or a mixture of dirt and play sand are excellent burial sites.

4. Support for temperature control;

Your Horsfield Tortoise's temperature regulation is influenced by its substrate. It should effectively maintain heat in the oven area while allowing for good cooling in other parts of the garden. A substance with good thermal properties helps the turtle to have a good body temperature.

5. Non-toxic and non-hazardous:

Make sure the substrate you choose is safe and non-toxic for your Horsfield Tortoise. Substances treated with chemicals or pesticides should be avoided. Natural ingredients with no additives or fragrances are ideal to avoid any negative effects on your turtle's health.

6. Ease of cleaning;

A clean environment is critical to the health of the Horsfield tortoise. Choose an easy-to-use filter to remove dirt and uneaten food as quickly as possible. Considerations such as filtering or simplifying contribute to the overall cleanliness of the room.

7. Stay away from fine dust;
Fine dust particles produced by the elements can endanger your turtle's respiratory system. It is possible to breathe good dust when digging or digging. To maintain the respiratory health of your Horsefield Tortoise, choose materials with low dust emissions.

8. Size and age of your turtle:
The size and age of your Horsfield tortoise will determine the mat you choose. Young turtles can benefit from soft and easy to dig soils, but adults can tolerate rough soil. As your turtle matures, you can make changes to the substrate.

9. Subsoil depth;

Consider the appropriate depth in the enclosure. A depth of at least 4-6 inches allows for good burying and digging. If this depth is desired, it helps to maintain the moisture level in a certain region, for example, as a specific moisture mask.

10. Combination of elements;

A balanced and rich environment can be created by combining different surfaces. For example, a mix of coconut bark and cypress mulch provides softness and structure. Experimenting with substrate combinations allows you to adjust the enclosure to your Horsfield turtle's taste.

11. Maintaining temperature;

The heat-retaining element contributes to the overall temperature increase in the environment. This is especially true in a humid region, where the surface must help provide a warm and pleasant environment for the turtle to maintain its body temperature.

12. Avoid using cedar and pine:

Avoid using cedar or pine shavings because the aromatic compounds and oils are harmful to rodents. To keep your Horsefield tortoise healthy, use tortoise-safe substrates such as cypress mulch, coconut husks, or organic topsoil.

13. Appearance during childbirth;

Choosing a tile that matches the look of the natural world will enhance the overall aesthetic of the fence. Natural-looking surfaces, such as sandy or earthy tones, create an attractive environment for both the turtle and the keeper.

14. Access to feeding:

Consider the nutrient availability of the subsoil. Too much loose material can make it difficult for your turtle to find and eat food. Defining feed zones within feeding zones or using a substrate with a slightly coarser texture can help reduce this problem.

15. Gradual Substrate Change:

When switching to a new tile, make adjustments gradually. Unexpected changes can be stressful for your Horsfield Tortoise. Mix the new tile with the old one over time until the transition is over. Watch for signs of stress in your turtle during this adjustment period.

16. Bioactive ingredients:

Bioactive ingredients, which include living organisms such as beneficial bacteria and springtails, provide additional benefits. These nutrients help decompose waste and create a more dynamic habitat for your

Horsfield Tortoise, contributing to a self-sustaining ecosystem in the backyard.

17. Humidity and humidity;

Although Horsfield's Tortoises prefer dry conditions, some may use high humidity in isolation to survive. Include wet hides or wet mats in the designated area to give the turtle options. Monitoring humidity levels benefits your pet's overall health.

18. Compatibility with Additional Enhancements:

Consider the component's compatibility with other boosters in the enclosure. Excavating and excavating the properties complement features such as climbing structures, shelters and boarding areas, thereby creating a suitable and stimulating environment.

19. PRICE AND AVAILABILITY:

Consider the cost and availability of the material, especially if you have a large enclosure or need to change it regularly. Choosing pads that are widely available and affordable makes the ongoing maintenance of the enclosure more reasonable.

20. DIY Substrates vs. Trade accessories:
Decide whether you want commercially available substrates or prefer to create a DIY mix. Commercial accessories are generally prepackaged and of consistent quality, but DIY options allow for customization based on your turtle's needs.

21. Investigate the behavior of a turtle:
Note the habits and preferences of the Horsefield Tortoise. Some turtles may have a preference for some substitutes over others. Observing how they interact with the retailer will allow you to tailor the pantry to their specific preferences.

22. Ovipositor;

If you have a female Horsfield tortoise, provide an appropriate replacement for egg laying. A mixture of organic soil and sand works well to build a nesting area. Make sure that the depth of the soil is sufficient to bury the eggs, to reduce the chance of egg-related problems.

23. Repair and Replacement;

Schedule regular maintenance and regularly assess the condition of the component. Damage to turtle growth and activity, soil contamination, or changes over time may require nutrient replacement. Monitoring the quality of the ingredients ensures a clean and comfortable living space.

24. Consultation with Reptile Veterinarian:

If you are confused about the best replacement for your Horsefield Tortoise or if your pet has any health problems, consult a reptile vet. Professional veterinarians specializing in reptile care can provide tailored recommendations based on your turtle's needs.

25. Continue your education.

Keep up with changes in substrate options and substrate care. Continuous education ensures that you can change and provide the best habitat for your Horsfield Tortoise as new products and research are developed.

In conclusion, choosing the right replacement for your Horsfield Tortoise is an important part of providing responsible and careful care. By considering things like drainage, safety, natural habitat conditions, and personal preferences, you can create a room that meets your turtle's physical and behavioral needs. Regular monitoring and substrate adjustments will improve the Horsefield Tortoise's overall health and well-being, allowing your pet to enjoy a happy and healthy life in captivity.

Chapter 9

Building a close relationship with your Horsefield Tortoise (Agrionemys horsfieldii or Testudo horsfieldii) can be rewarding and fun. Although turtles are not naturally sociable creatures like dogs or cats, they bond with the people they care for. Building a relationship with your Horsfield Tortoise requires learning about their unique activities, engaging in meaningful activities, and creating an environment that promotes safety and trust. In this comprehensive tutorial, we'll explore different socialization and bonding techniques to help you bond with your adorable Horsfield Turtles.

1. Understanding turtle behavior:

Before starting the community process with a Horsfield Tortoise, it is important to understand their natural behavior. Horseshoe turtles are typically solitary and independent creatures. Unlike more sociable pets, they may not actively seek out social interactions. You can still form bonds based on trust and fun experiences.

2. Respecting their personal space:

Respecting the Horsfield Tortoise's personal space is an important part of interacting with them. Turtles may not like handling or petting like mammals do. Avoid using force when the turtle approaches you and let them come at their own pace. Building trust requires an understanding of their boundaries and patience.

3. Consistent attendance:

You should regularly spend quality time with your Horsefield Tortoise. Sit close to their seat, speak in a calm voice, and do quiet movements. With your presence, you help people become familiar with your company and associate it with positive events.

4. Feeding by hand;

Hand feeding your Horsfield Tortoise is a great way to get them used to your presence. Serve them on hand with your favorite leafy greens or turtle-friendly bits of fruit. This allows them to identify your presence with food while developing a positive interaction.

5. Creating a pattern:

Setting a schedule will help the Horsefield tortoise feel more comfortable. A regular schedule provides stability and is often well received by turtles who respond well to patterns that match their natural functions. This can be applied to daily habits, daily observations or specific activities.

6. When should you go outside the container?

Allowing your Horsfield Tortoise to seek out a safe and supervised area outside the fence will increase the enjoyment of bonding with them. Make sure there are no potential hazards and that the area is an escape. At this level of exploration, you can move freely, which can encourage natural activities.

7. Looking at natural features

Take time to observe and enjoy your Horsefield Tortoise's natural habits. Knowing their natural habits and needs will strengthen your bond with them, whether they are browsing, sunbathing, or digging. To create a more complete and rich environment, build an enclosure that supports these organic features.

8. Encourage constructively:

Positive reinforcement will help you form a strong bond with your Horsfield Tortoise. When they exhibit desired behaviors, such as coming to you or responding to cues, positive reinforcement can take the form of soft praise, a soothing voice, or a favorite reward. This increases the connection between your presence and positive experiences.

9. Avoid sudden movements:

Turtles can be frightened by loud noises or sudden movements. When interacting with your Horsefield Tortoise, move slowly and carefully. They may be frightened by sudden movements, resulting in tension or avoidance. A calm and gentle approach contributes to a positive and stress-free atmosphere.

10. Develop good handling habits:

While some turtles can tolerate handling with time and positive experiences, not all will enjoy it. If handling is necessary, make sure it is painless and gentle. Make sure they are supporting their body adequately, not moving too quickly, and paying attention to any signs of stress or discomfort.

11. Gradually establish trust

It takes time to build trust with a Horsfield tortoise. Allow them to adjust to your presence at their own pace. Instead of rushing conversations, focus on creating meaningful connections. Faith is built on positive, patient and consistent rhymes.

12. Interactive Upgrade:

Incorporate interactive enrichment activities into your Horsfield Turtle routine. Providing puzzle feeders, hiding goodies in places to look for, or introducing them to new items can all help. These mental exercises will help young people make better connections between their environment and your involvement.

13. Touch and touch gently:

Some turtles may not mind being handled or stroked, while others may. If your Horsefield Tortoise appears to be amenable to handling, try petting its head or shell a little. Always watch how they react, and stop if they show any signs of stress.

14. Recognize individual differences:-

Horseshoe tortoises, like all other creatures, have unique characteristics. Some people may be more reserved while others may be more outgoing and inquisitive. Recognize and respect these differences by tailoring your strategy to their personal preferences and comfort zones.

15. Outside of Safe Contacts:

If your climate allows, it may be worth providing your Horsfield tortoise with safe outdoor activities. They can be exposed to a variety of environmental stimuli, sunlight and fresh air in a safe outdoor enclosure or during supervised outdoor exploration sessions.

16. Setting up a safe place;

Make sure your Horsefield Tortoise has places to hide or retreat to where they feel safe. Having a place to go when they need a break increases their overall sense of security and comfort.

17. Speaking and Singing Signs:

Turtles may learn to recognize your voice, even if they don't respond to vocal cues or noisy pets. Use a calm, quiet voice when communicating with the Horsfield Tortoise. Over time, you may begin to associate your voice with positive things.

18. Vigilant monitoring of stress indicators

Watch for signs of stress in your Horsfield Tortoise. Signs of stress may include changes in behavior, rapid breathing, or withdrawal. If stress is found, assess the environment for potential stressors and make the necessary improvements.

19. Avoid overcrowding.

Some turtles tolerate touching, but excessive handling should be avoided. Turtles, in general, feel more at peace in their environment, and regular handling can create discomfort. Focus on alternative positive engagement methods and save handling for emergencies.

20. Scent Detection:

To build associations, introduce pleasant associations with familiar smells. Keep a scented item of clothing nearby when the turtle eats or explores. This will help them get used to your presence and scent.

21. Watching a quiet moment:

Horsfield tortoises, like all reptiles, need rest from time to time. Respect their sleeping time and do not disturb them when they dig or escape to hiding places.

Providing them with a calm and peaceful environment during these times will improve their overall well-being.

22. Veterinary treatment and integrity;

Regular vet care can affect the Horsefield Tortoise's level of trust in you as its caretaker. Regular veterinary check-ups ensure that their health is monitored and any potential concerns are dealt with as soon as possible. This constant attention shows how committed you are to their safety.

23. Bonding with shared space activities:

Include regular exercise in which your Horsefield Tortoise participates. Whether it's feeding, changing their water, or snuggling with their litter box, these daily activities encourage positive interactions and build your overall bond.

24. Scheduled Observation Periods:-

Watch your Horsefield Tortoise for a while. By recording your observations, you can learn more about their habits, preferences, and distinguishing characteristics. A deliberate approach allows you to get to know and understand your reproductive partner better.

25. Long term commitment and patience:
Building a close relationship with your Horsfield Tortoise takes time, patience and understanding. Because each turtle is unique, the time it takes to build rapport and trust can vary. Think of the process as continuous growth and lasting friendships.

26. Respecting Boundaries;
Understand and respect boundaries when dealing with a Horsfield tortoise. They may not show the same obvious signs of affection as friendly pets, but they can still form friendships and express affection in their own unique

ways. Knowing and accepting these limitations will facilitate an enjoyable and stress-free relationship.

27. Creating a positive relationship with management:
When handling your Horsefield Tortoise, focus on developing a positive relationship. Give treats before and after handling and make sure the process is calm and smooth. You may associate handling slowly with good things.

28. Promoting turtle-safe friendships:
Horsfield tortoises can occasionally live happily with other tortoises. When considering a mate, gradually introduce turtle-safe people and monitor their interactions. This can lead to more stimulation and social opportunities.

29. Comparison of outdoor activities:

If your Horsefield Tortoise likes to explore the outdoors, consider doing outdoor activities with them. Sit close by and let them graze or explore at their own pace. Spending time outdoors with your turtle can help strengthen your bond.

30. Bond Travel Document:-
Keeping a journal of your bonding journey will help you track your progress and keep track of your time with Horsfield's Tortoise. Capturing recent events through photographs, movies, or a simple journal can help create long-lasting memories.

In conclusion, getting to know and become acquainted with Horsfield's Tortoise is a unique and gradual process that requires tolerance, understanding and a commitment to their well-being. By treating these amazing reptiles with respect, encouraging positive interactions, and providing an engaging environment, you can create strong, long-lasting bonds. Remember that relationships can be tricky, and building trust and friendship is a fun process that takes time.

Chapter 10

Breeding Tips: Breeding Strategies for Successful Horsfield Tortoises

Breeding horsfield tortoises, also known as Testudo horsfieldii or Agrionemys horsfieldii, is an exciting yet responsible activity. These robust, small tortoises from the arid regions of Central Asia exhibit distinct characteristics during breeding season. A detailed understanding of the unique characteristics of Horsefield Tortoises, as well as the provision of favorable conditions for mating, mating and egg laying are all required for successful breeding. This comprehensive guide will give you all the knowledge you need to successfully breed Horsfield tortoises and maintain the health of adults and hatchlings.

1. Age and Maturity:

It is critical for optimal breeding that both male and female Horsfield tortoises are of acceptable age and development. Female turtles should be kept for 5-7 years, and males should be kept for 4-6 years. Premature breeding can result in eggs with low viability and health problems.

2. Health Assessment:

Before starting the breeding process, properly assess the health of the breeding pair. This includes a vet exam to make sure they are healthy and have no underlying medical issues. Preventing health problems early helps in an efficient and stress-free reproductive process.

3. Sleep Process and Periods:-

Horsfield tortoises are affected by seasonal cycles, and environmental cues often trigger their reproductive behavior. Provide different periods to mimic their native habitat, including hibernation or hibernation. This seasonal variation helps maintain their reproductive cycle and regulates reproductive hormones.

4. Environmental Indicators:

Create environmental cues that closely approximate the natural conditions of the breeding season. Changes in UVB exposure, daylight hours and temperature are all included. By changing these environmental conditions, we can tell the turtles when it's time to court and mate.

5. Special Enclosures:-

If you have more than one, separate breeding pairs of Horseshoe Field Tortoises into separate enclosures during mating season. This reduces the possibility of stress situations and allows you to pay attention to how you work. Also, keeping turtles away can prevent violent conflicts during breeding season.

6. Looking at dating features:

Horsfield tortoises engage in courtship behavior especially during the breeding season. Head shaking, turning, and light shaking are examples of these actions. By observing these courtship actions, it is possible to know that the turtles are ready to mate. Patience is required as not all matings are successful mating attempts.

7. Mating Patterns:-

Horsfield tortoises must mount the female to mate successfully. During breeding, this operation can happen more than once in a short period of time. While mating behavior is often noticeable, it's important to keep an eye on things and make sure neither turtle is showing signs of stress or illness.

8. Creating a nesting site:

Prepare a suitable place in the incubator for the female to build a nest and lay her eggs. The substrate around the nest should be a mix of sand and loam that can be easily dug. Make sure the foundation is 6 to 8 inches deep to bury the eggs.

9. Burying and laying eggs;
Female Horsfield tortoises typically drop a clutch of eggs after a successful mating attempt. After the eggs are laid, the female bury them in the prepared nest. Allow this process to complete without intervention. Do not disturb the nest to protect the eggs from stress and to keep them where they are.

10. Collecting and dipping eggs;
If you choose to monitor and manage the hatching process, carefully remove the eggs after they are laid. When collecting the eggs, be careful not to change or drop them. Place the eggs in an incubator that satisfies the necessary parameters such as stable humidity and temperature. Monitor the incubation period closely.

11. Incubation temperature;

Maintain a temperature of 82°F to 88°F (28°C to 31°C). The temperature in this region can affect the sex of the chick. Males are usually produced in cooler temperatures, but females are more often produced in warmer conditions. Maintaining a consistent temperature is critical to a healthy embryo.

12. Incubating substance:-

Use a mixture of vermiculite and water or any other suitable substrate for the eggs. This substance provides the necessary moisture for egg development. Monitor moisture content to avoid dehydration or high humidity, both of which affect egg viability.

13. Incubation period:

Horsfield tortoise eggs typically take between sixty and ninety days to hatch. During this time, check the eggs for any anomalies or signs of mold or fungus. If the eggs are colored or have a strange smell, there may be a problem that needs to be solved immediately.

14. Making a forest enclosure:-

As soon as the eggs hatch, give the chicks their own enclosure. This enclosure should feature appropriate basements, hiding places, hatches, and access to UVB lighting. Make the environment, especially the heat sinks, suitable for the mud's special needs.

15. Watering and feeding first:

Hatching horseshoe turtles must have access to clean water to drink and bathe. Feed your child a diet rich in vegetables, leafy greens, and calcium supplements. Monitor their diet and adjust the diet as needed to promote their growth and development.

16. Social dynamics of young animals

If you have more than one brood, explore their social dynamics. Although Horsfield Tortoises prefer to live alone, they can tolerate the company of other turtles at first. However, it's important to be on the lookout for any signs of stress or hostility and be ready to extinguish them if necessary.

17. Monitoring growth and development;
Monitor the chick's growth and development closely. Note their height, weight and general health. Frequent vet check-ups are required to ensure the safety of the hatchlings and to address any health issues as soon as possible.

18. Maintaining a proper diet:
Provide nutritious and nutritious food to hungry adults and chicks. In particular, calcium is needed to form strong shells. Talk to a reptile-specific veterinarian to

develop an appropriate diet for Horsefield tortoises at different life stages.

19. How to Prevent Fertility:-

If you want to breed Horsfield Tortoises in different seasons, monitor the pairs regularly to avoid inbreeding. Maintaining genealogical records and avoiding re-interbreeding of closely related individuals can help preserve genetic diversity and reduce the risk of health problems in future generations.

20. Improving the Hatchling Environment;

Allow chicks to engage in natural activities and exploration to improve their environment. Add rough objects, shallow water dishes and small hiding places to the bottom. Environmental enrichment improves the chicks' overall well-being and behavioral development.

21. Evacuation of Incubation Area:-

As the bushes grow, gradually remove them from the sheltered area. This requires bringing normal humidity and temperature to the enclosure. Monitor how they behave as the environment changes and adjust as necessary to maximize their health.

22. Cleanliness and Cleaning;

Maintain clean and sanitary conditions for both hatchlings and breeding adults. To prevent the development of parasites and bacteria, clean feeding areas, water bowls and cages regularly. The overall health and well-being of the turtles depends on adequate hygiene.

23. Continue your education.

Keep abreast of new developments in veterinary medicine, breeding methods and reptile care. Continuing education ensures your ability to adapt and provide everything possible for Horsfield's tortoises throughout their lives, from breeding to caring for their young.

24. Participation in community activities;

Connect with the reptile community and ask for advice from experienced breeders. Participating in discussions with knowledgeable people, visiting reptile displays, and participating in forums can provide valuable perspectives and information for good horse field tortoise breeding.

25. Appropriate Position and Ownership;

Before starting a breeding business, consider ownership obligations as well as hatchery or reintroduction. Make sure you have a responsible ownership strategy, including partnering with reputable reptile enthusiasts or finding chick-friendly homes.

26. Consider the following legal issues:

Know and follow all laws and regulations governing the ownership and breeding of Horsefield tortoises. Regional laws, licensing or sales and breeding restrictions may apply. Understanding and commitment to these guidelines is required for ethical breeding methods.

27. Keeping records;

Keep detailed information about the breeding process, including mating dates, egg laying dates, hatching conditions and hatching details. Accurate documentation can help evaluate the effectiveness of breeding efforts, monitor the welfare of turtles, and encourage careful breeding practices.

28. Genetic differences:

Consider how important racial diversity is to breeding efforts. Avoid close relationships as a couple to avoid depression. Conservation of diverse genetic pools affects the overall health and strength of the Horsefield tortoise population.

29. Veterinary services;

Establish a relationship with a veterinarian who specializes in reptiles and tortoises. A frequent vet can help detect health problems early and ensure that the pups you want, especially during breeding, get the care they need.

30. Enjoying the journey:

Horsfield tortoises breed with careful monitoring, guidance and control. Enjoy watching these amazing reptiles in their natural habitat while supporting their life cycle and increasing their quality of life. It's the right balancing act between science, observation and a genuine respect for these amazing turtles that makes successful breeding so much fun.

In conclusion, horsefield tortoise breeding requires thorough preparation, knowledge of the animal's natural behavior, and a commitment to responsible ownership. You can help the health and conservation of this amazing species by learning about its unique characteristics, preparing breeding conditions, and taking an active role in everything from care to mating. Remember that every successful breeding event demonstrates the commitment of the keeper, and that ethical breeding practices contribute to the overall well-being and sustainability of captive reptile populations.

Questions to be asked

Q: What is the scientific name of the Horsefield Tortoise?

A: The scientific name of the Horsefield Tortoise is Testudo horsfieldii.

Q: How long do Horsefield tortoises generally live?

A: With proper care, Horsefield tortoises can live for 75 or 100 years.

Q: How big is an average Horsefield tortoise?

A: The shell length of an adult Horsfield's tortoise is 6 to 10 inches (15 to 25 cm).

Q: What is the native habitat of the Horsfield Tortoise?

A: Horsfield tortoises are native to Central Asia, including populations in Turkmenistan, Uzbekistan, Kazakhstan, and Russia.

Q: What temperature is ideal for a Horsfield Tortoise enclosure?

A: The temperature in the Horsfield Tortoise's home should be between 75 and 85°F (24 and 29°C) during the day, dropping slightly at night.

Q: How often should I provide a scratching post for my Horsfield Tortoise?

A: Provide a temperature controlled room at 90-100°F (32-38°C) for 12-14 hours per day.

Q: What type of flooring works best in a Horsfield tortoise enclosure?

A: A mixture of earth, coconut coir and cypress mulch is ideal for Horsfield tortoises.

Q: Can you keep Horsfield Tortoises outdoors?

A: Horsefield tortoises can be kept outside with shade and sunlight if the weather permits.

Q: What kind of food should a Horsfield tortoise eat?

A: A Horsfield Tortoise's diet should include grasses, high-fiber vegetables, and sometimes fruits.

Q: Do Horsfield Tortoises Need More Calcium?

A: Calcium supplements help Horsfield tortoises keep their shells healthy. Give them some calcium powder or chopped bones with dinner.

Q: Can Horsefield Tortoises be fed commercial tortoise pellets?

A: Tortoise pellets are acceptable, but should not be the sole source of food for these animals. Weeds and fresh greens are important for their health.

Q: How often should I bathe my Horsfield Tortoise?

A: A weekly bath should be sufficient for your Horsfield Tortoise. Make sure the water is warm and shallow.

Q: Can Horsfield Tortoises Sleep?

A: Horsfield tortoises hibernate in the wild. However, hibernation is not recommended for turtles kept in captivity unless strictly supervised.

Q: How do I know what gender my Horsfield Tortoise is?

A: Male Horsfield tortoises have a long tail and a convex plastron, while females have a short tail and a flat or slightly convex plastron.

Q: Horsfield turtles need a friend?

A: Horsfield tortoises like to live alone, so it's best to keep them that way to avoid stress and competition.

Q: What foods are safe for Horsfield tortoises?

A: Safe plants include edible weeds, clover, hibiscus leaves and dandelion greens. Avoid poisonous plants.

Q: Can tortoises swim?

A: Despite their ability to swim, horseshoe crabs are not very good swimmers. Check them at any time and make sure the water is shallow.

Q: How do I provide UVB light for my Horsefield Tortoise?

A: It is best to use a UVB lamp designed for reptiles. Make sure the turtle gets ten to twelve hours of sunlight a day.

Horseshoe tortoises can be kept as pets or in groups with other reptiles.

A: Horsfield tortoises have special care requirements that may differ from other animals, so it is not recommended to keep them with other pets.

Q: Do Horsfield tortoises dig burrows?

A: It is true that Horsefield Tortoises dig burrows to escape from overheated conditions.

Q: What is shingles in horses, and how can I prevent it in horses?

A: Shell rot is caused by bacteria or fungi on the shell. To prevent shell rot, keep the area clean, provide adequate moisture and treat any damage as soon as possible.

Q: How often should I clean my Horsefield Tortoise enclosure?

A: Clean up any food scraps or droppings daily. After cleaning carefully, change the pad every four to six weeks.

Q: Can Horsfield turtles be kept in glass aquariums?

A: Glass tanks are not the best housing choice for Horsfield turtles because they provide little air flow. Well-ventilated enclosures are recommended.

Q: What kind of respiratory infection symptoms can a Horsfield tortoise show?

A: Symptoms include shortness of breath, difficulty breathing, runny nose and fatigue. If you experience any of these symptoms, contact your veterinarian.

Q: How can I build an outdoor room big enough for my Horsefield Tortoise?

A: Make sure the enclosure has a sunny and shady spot, build strong fences, build shelter and grow turtle-safe plants.

Q: My turtle is a Horsfield turtle. Can a heat pad be used in it?

A: Heating mats, while useful, are not the primary source of heat. Make a baking place out of the above-mentioned heat bulbs.

Q: What should I do if my Horsfield Tortoise stops eating?

A: Watch for symptoms, monitor temperature and ensure adequate lighting. If the condition persists, consult a veterinarian.

Q: What should I do to teach a hand-fed Horsfield tortoise to eat?

A: Practice patience and feed food from your hand frequently. The turtle may come to associate your hand with interesting things.

Q: Is it possible to keep Horsfield Tortoises completely indoors?

A: Although they can be confined indoors, it is better for their health to allow them some outdoor time, especially during the summer.

Q: Can Horsfield Tortoises be toilet trained?

A: Potty training Horsefield tortoises is not the same as potty training other pets. The enclosure should be cleaned regularly.

Q: What do I do in a Horsfield tortoise bed?

A: Use dirt, coconut husks and cypress mulch in your substrate mix to create a warm, organic bedding.

Q: How can I prevent my Horsfield Tortoise's beak from growing too long?

A: Provide a variety of foods, including those that should be eaten, as well as a cut bone for natural beak dressing.

Q: Do Horsfield Tortoises Like To Be Treated?

A: Horsfield tortoises generally do not like to be handled, but they are tolerant. Reduce your handling to relieve stress.

Q: Can Horsfield Tortoises Be Grouped?

A: Horsfield tortoises can be housed in groups if the enclosure is large enough to accommodate them, as long as aggressive behavior is not monitored.

Q: How do I create a moist hide for my Horsfield Tortoise?

A: hide box filled with moist sphagnum moss can be used to make a moist mulch.

A: Is it necessary to increase the temperature in the enclosure where Horsfield tortoises live?

A: Thermal expansion can be achieved by establishing a cold zone in the low 70s°F (about 21°C) and between 90 and 100°F (32 and 38°C).

Horsfield tortoises can eat iceberg lettuce.

A: Although not dangerous, iceberg lettuce has little nutritional value. Eat a variety of dark and leafy vegetables for maximum nutrition.

Q: How can I prevent my shaking Horsefield tortoise from falling apart?

A: To avoid tipping over, make sure the nesting area is flat and easy for the turtle to access.

Q: Do Horsefield tortoises prefer day or night?

A: Horsfield turtles are diurnal species, meaning they are active during the day.

Q: How can I provide a safe outdoor enclosure for my Horsefield Tortoise?

A: Use secure fencing to avoid waterlogging, provide predator-proof cover and ensure proper drainage in the area.

Horsfield tortoises can live with other tortoises indoors.

Q: What can I do to prevent my Horsfield Tortoise from becoming overweight?

Answer: To prevent obesity, monitor their diet, avoid more fruits and provide a variety of nutritious foods.

Q: Are tomatoes safe for Horsfield tortoises?

A: Despite their high acid content, tomatoes can be eaten in moderation. Offer ripe tomatoes as a treat every now and then.

What can I do to convince my Horsfield Tortoise to eat more leafy vegetables?

A: Serve a variety of greens, finely chopped or chopped, and pair with favorite foods to increase acceptance.

Can Horsfield Tortoises Eat Only Canned Food?

A turtle's diet should not only consist of store-bought foods. Include more fresh greens, vegetables and sometimes fruits in your diet for a balanced diet.

Can Horsfield Tortoises Eat Store-Bought Cactus Pads?

A: You can safely eat store-bought nopales.

Can Horsefield Tortoises Eat Mushrooms?

A: While some mushrooms are safe, some are dangerous, so it is better to avoid them. Use only vegetables and safe greens.

Are Carrots Safe for Horsefield Tortoises to Feed?

A: Carrots are high in beta-carotene but can be eaten in moderation. Feed regularly as a treat.

Can Horsefield Tortoises Eat Parsley?

A: Parsley, because of its high calcium-phosphorus ratio, is good to give them occasionally, but should not be their main source of nutrition.

How can I upgrade my Horsefield Turtle?

A: To make their environment interesting, provide different objects to study, change the texture of the fence and change the hiding places.